All About Your
Skeleton

113762

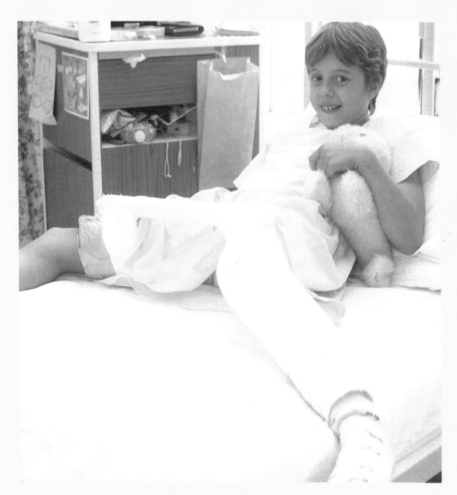

Donna Bailey

STECK-VAUGHN
L I B R A R Y
A Division of Steck-Vaughn Company

Austin, Texas

How to Use This Book

This book tells you many things about the bones that make up your skeleton. There is a Table of Contents on the next page. It shows you what each double page of the book is about. For example, pages 10 and 11 tell you about "How We Move."

On many of these pages you will find some words that are printed in **bold** type. The bold type shows you that these words are in the Glossary on pages 46 and 47. The Glossary explains the meaning of some words that may be new to you.

At the very end of the book there is an Index. The Index tells you where to find certain words in the book. For example, you can use it to look up words like fibula, joints, cartilage, and marrow, and many other words to do with your skeleton and bones.

Printed and bound in the United States of America
1 2 3 4 5 6 7 8 9 0 LB 95 94 93 92

Library of Congress Cataloging-In-Publication Data

Bailey, Donna.
    All about your skeleton / Donna Bailey.
      p. cm. — (Health facts)
    Includes index.
    Summary: Describes the structure and function of the human skeletal system.
     ISBN 0-8114-2780-3
     1. Human skeleton—Juvenile literature. [1. Skeleton.]
I. Title. II. Series: Bailey, Donna. Health facts.
QM101.B34 1991
611'.71—dc20
                                        90-10114
                                          CIP AC

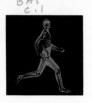

Contents

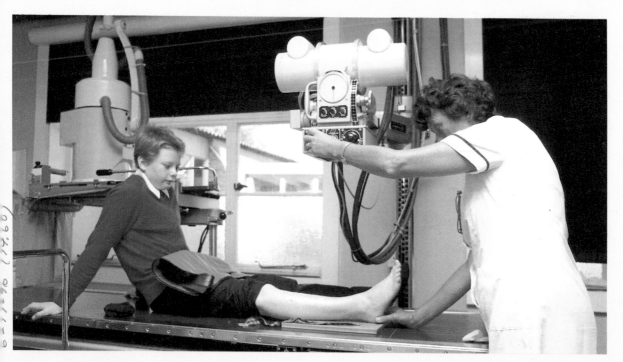

Introduction

cormorant

jellyfish

crab

A crab's body is held together by its hard outer shell. A jellyfish has no shell and no bones. Its soft body is supported by the water. Birds, humans, reptiles, and fish all have a skeleton to support their bodies.

If you press your skin, you can feel many hard bones underneath it. Your bones protect the soft parts of your body such as your heart and lungs.

Our bones are joined together by different joints that let us move. **Muscles** fixed to the bones can pull the bones in different directions to make the movements.

Bones and muscles work together to make us move.

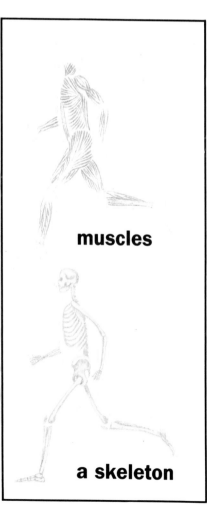

muscles

a skeleton

Learning About the Body

Long ago people knew that putting on **splints** helped a broken bone to mend properly. They did not know how the skeleton and muscles work together, and how we move.

this frog is using the muscles in his back legs to jump

6

The first book about the structure of the human body was written by a Belgian scientist 400 years ago. Then, 200 years later, an Italian doctor discovered that electricity made the leg of a dead frog twitch.

Many years later, scientists discovered that **nerves** carry messages to and from the **brain.** These messages tell our muscles how and when to move.

The first photographs and films made it easier for scientists to look at each tiny movement and see how muscles and bones work together.

The Skeleton

An adult has 206 bones, all joined to make up a skeleton. Bones are made of millions of tiny **cells.**

The hard outer layer of a bone protects the spongy bone inside. The **marrow,** where **red blood cells** are made, is in the center of the bone. The ends of the bones are protected by tough, rubbery **cartilages.**

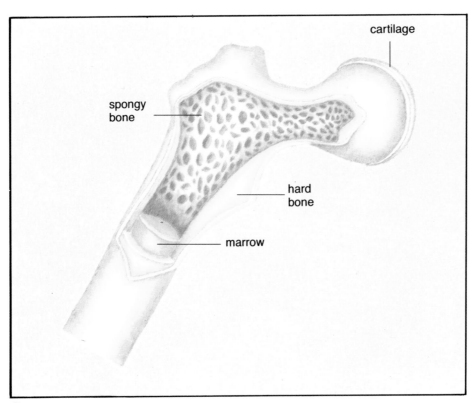

the skeleton

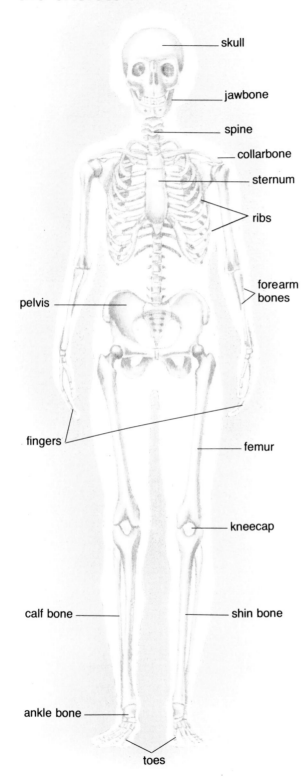

- skull
- jawbone
- spine
- collarbone
- sternum
- ribs
- forearm bones
- pelvis
- fingers
- femur
- kneecap
- calf bone
- shin bone
- ankle bone
- toes

All our bones have names. Your **skull** protects your brain, and your **ribs** protect the heart and lungs in your chest.

The longest bone, the femur or thigh bone, is about 20 inches long in a person who is 6 feet tall. The smallest bone, the **stirrup** inside your ear, is only 1/10 inch long.

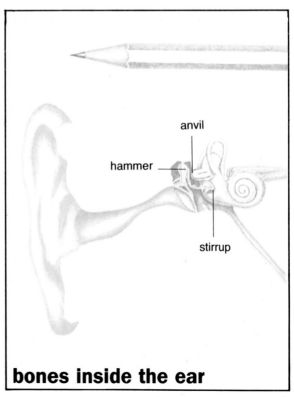

- anvil
- hammer
- stirrup

bones inside the ear

9

How We Move

Your brain controls everything you think, feel, or do. Messages from different muscles reach different parts of the brain.

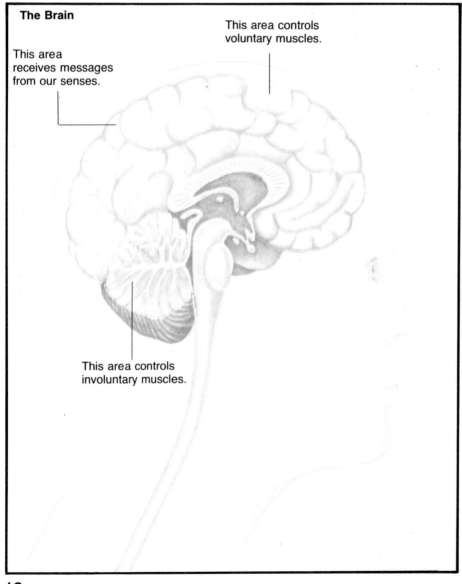

The Brain

This area receives messages from our senses.

This area controls voluntary muscles.

This area controls involuntary muscles.

the brain controls the movements of the muscles

When we run or skip, we think about what we are doing, and our brains decide what movements to make. The brain then sends messages along the nerves to our arms and legs. The muscles here are called **voluntary** muscles because they work when we tell them to.

We use voluntary muscles when chewing and swallowing our food. After that, **involuntary** muscles take over to help us **digest** the food.

11

Body Connections

Our bones are joined by different joints. **Ball-and-socket joints,** like those in the hips and shoulders, can move in almost any direction. **Hinge joints,** like those in the elbows, knees, fingers, and toes, can only move backward and forward. **Gliding joints,** like those in our wrists and ankles, can bend and turn. The movement of the joints are controlled by **ligaments.**

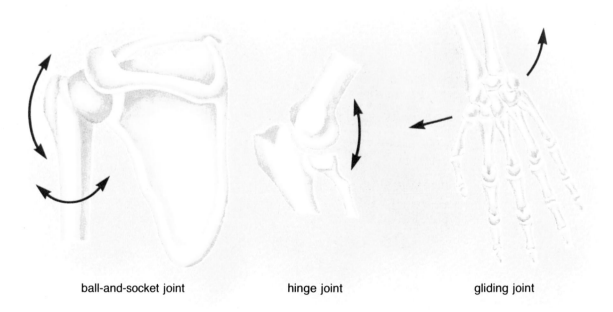

ball-and-socket joint   hinge joint   gliding joint

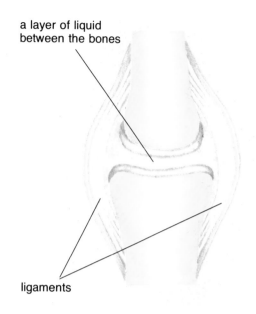

a layer of liquid between the bones

ligaments

In some joints there is a layer of liquid between the bones to stop them from rubbing together.

Between the joints of the **spine** are soft pads of cartilage which separate the bones and cushion the spine from any shocks.

The flat bones of the skull are joined together by **fibrous joints** which do not allow any movement.

Ligaments tie the joints together and hold the bones firmly in place.

bones of the spine

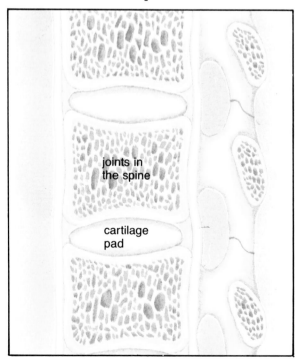

joints in the spine

cartilage pad

bones of the skull

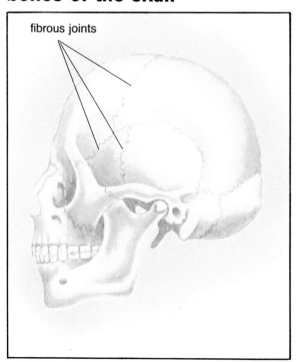

fibrous joints

Muscle Power

We make all our movements by using muscles. Your muscles are made up of bundles of thin fibers. Muscles are fixed to your bones by strong, tough cords called **tendons.**

Like your bones, all your muscles have names. For example, you have deltoids in the shoulders and biceps in the arms.

Muscles always work in groups or pairs. When we want to make a movement, the muscle shortens and bunches up. When we want to move in the opposite direction, another muscle shortens and the first muscle relaxes.

14

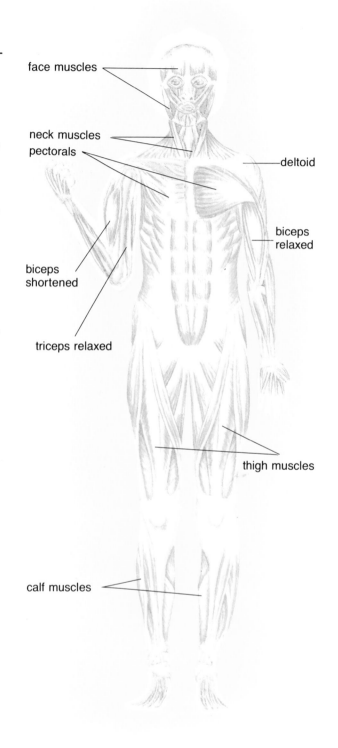

face muscles

neck muscles

pectorals

deltoid

biceps relaxed

biceps shortened

triceps relaxed

thigh muscles

calf muscles

Which muscles is the tennis player in the photo using as she serves? She is using her biceps and triceps to bend and straighten her arm. Her shoulder and chest muscles raise her arms high, and her calf and thigh muscles keep her body balanced.

biceps bulge during this arm-wrestling contest

The Skull

The **cranium** is made of smooth, curved bones that fit together.

the cranium
is shaped
like a crash
helmet

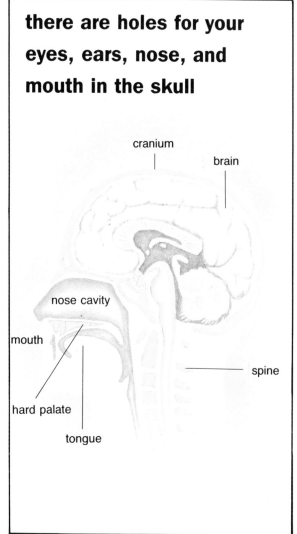

the bones of the skull make a box to protect the brain

joints

cranium

ear position

eye socket

upper jaw

teeth

lower jaw

there are holes for your eyes, ears, nose, and mouth in the skull

cranium

brain

nose cavity

mouth

hard palate

tongue

spine

The bones of the cranium and face do not move, except for the lower jawbone. Holes in the skull let **blood vessels** pass into the bottom of the skull. Nerves reach the brain through a hole at the back of the skull. Other gaps in the skull allow us to see, breathe, hear, and eat.

The Backbone

The spine of an adult is made up of 26 small bones called **vertebrae.** Seven of these vertebrae support the skull. The top vertebra is called the atlas and the second one is called the axis. The ribs join up to the next 12 vertebrae. The next five support the back muscles, and after these are five vertebrae which are joined together to form the sacrum. The last four vertebrae are also joined together and make the coccyx.

Each vertebra has a hole in the middle to make a channel for the **spinal cord** to go through. This joins the nerves to the brain.

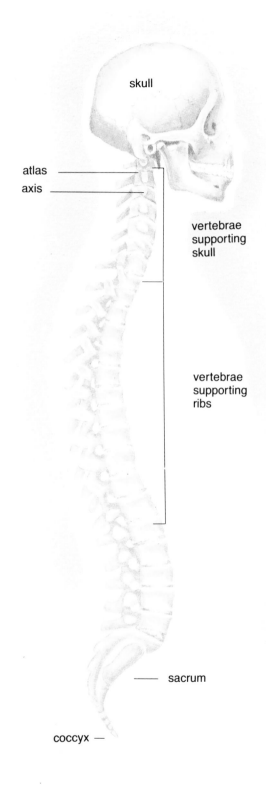

skull

atlas

axis

vertebrae supporting skull

vertebrae supporting ribs

sacrum

coccyx

The spinal cord is made of **gray** and **white matter.** Just as small roads branch off from a highway, so 31 pairs of nerves branch off from the spinal cord. The nerves send signals to control all our movements.

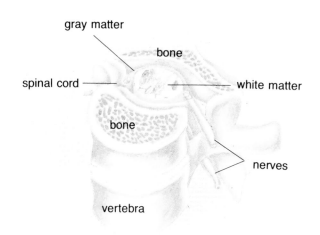

gray matter
bone
spinal cord
white matter
bone
nerves
vertebra

your spinal cord has branches somewhat like a highway

19

The Chest and Shoulders

Your twelve pairs of ribs form a strong cage to protect your heart and lungs. Your ribs are all joined to your spine at the back, but only the top seven pairs of ribs are joined to the sternum, or breast bone at the front of your chest.

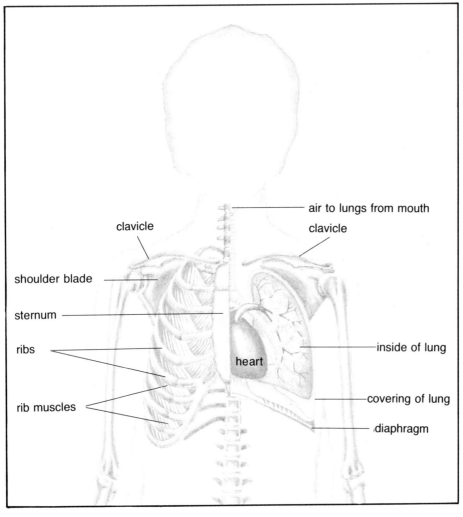

clavicle

air to lungs from mouth

clavicle

shoulder blade

sternum

ribs

inside of lung

heart

covering of lung

rib muscles

diaphragm

inside the chest

shoulder muscles can lift and carry heavy weights

Your shoulder muscles are fixed to two large, flat bones which are your shoulder blades.

In front, you can feel a long, thin bone going across to each shoulder. These bones are called clavicles or collarbones. Clavicles join your rib cage to your shoulders.

rugby players use their shoulders in the scrum

The Pelvis

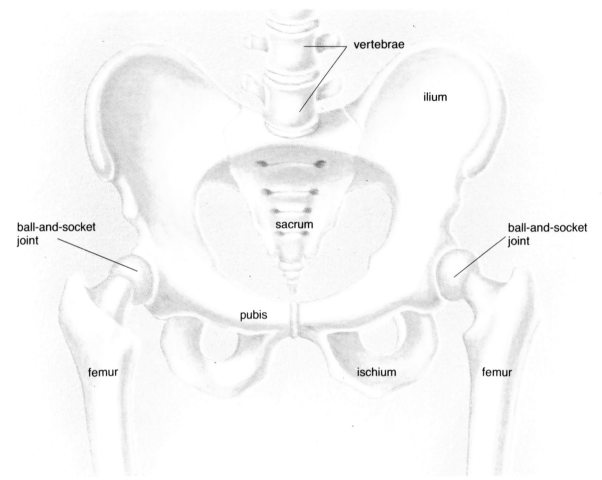

vertebrae

ilium

ball-and-socket
joint

sacrum

ball-and-socket
joint

pubis

femur

ischium

femur

Your pelvis supports your spine. Your pelvis also protects the soft inner parts of the lower half of your body. The sacrum joins your pelvis to the rest **of your** spine. The bones of the legs are **linked** to the pelvis by ball-and-socket joints.

A woman's pelvis is wider than a man's to give extra protection to the uterus, the part of a woman's body where a baby grows. When the baby is ready to be born, strong muscles in the uterus squeeze hard to push the baby out.

These women are doing exercises to make the pelvis muscles strong.

The Arms and Legs

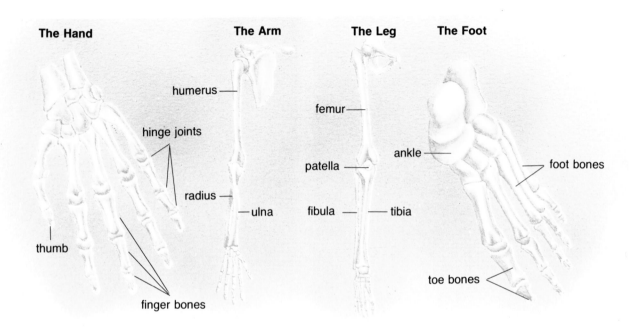

The Hand

thumb

hinge joints

finger bones

The Arm

humerus

radius

ulna

The Leg

femur

patella

fibula — tibia

ankle

The Foot

foot bones

toe bones

The small bones in our hands and feet help us to do delicate tasks.

The humerus is a big bone between the shoulder and the elbow. The **radius** and the **ulna** are thinner bones between the elbow and the wrist.

drawing Chinese letters
needs delicate movements

The femur is a big bone in the thigh. It is fixed to the thinner **tibia** and **fibula** bones by a hinge joint at the knee. This joint is protected by the kneecap or **patella.**

We use the bones in our legs to walk, run, play games, and dance. The young ballet dancers in the picture train hard to develop strong muscles in their calves, thighs, and feet.

Broken Bones

A broken bone is called a fracture.
The bone has to be set or held firmly
in the proper position so that it will
grow together correctly. The boy in
the picture is wearing a plaster cast
to keep his bones rigid.

bone cells are light and strong

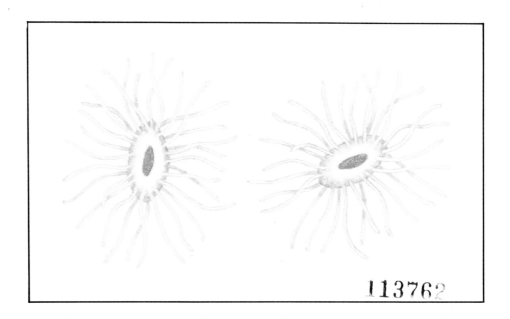

Broken bones heal by growing together again.

First the blood around the break hardens and covers the broken ends. **Minerals** seep out of the broken bones, which makes the broken ends get soft. Bone cells divide to make new bone called **callus.** The callus slowly closes the gap in the bones. Then it hardens until the bone is back to normal again.

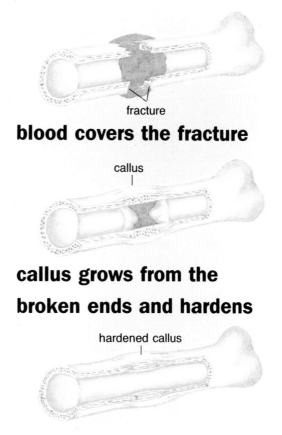

fracture

blood covers the fracture

callus

callus grows from the broken ends and hardens

hardened callus

How a Broken Bone Heals

Unable to Move

Sometimes the muscles around a fracture are so strong that they pull the broken bones apart again. Then **traction** is needed, using a weight to pull against the muscles so the broken ends stay together. The boy in this picture is being given traction for a broken leg.

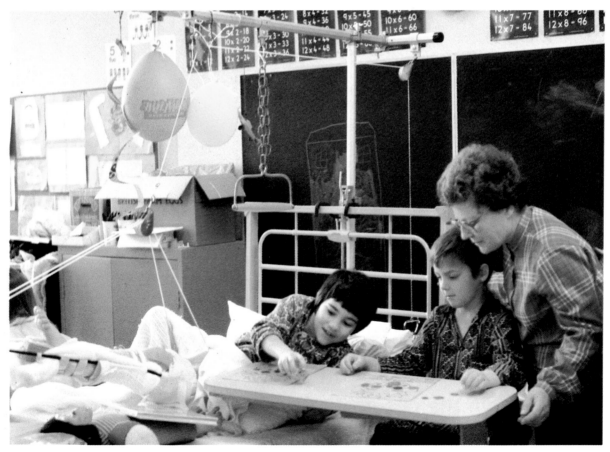

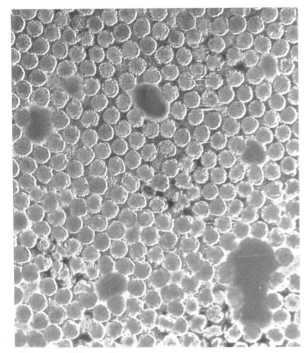

the polio virus

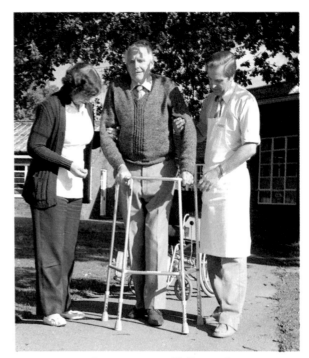

using a walking frame

Nerves in the spine may get damaged by a disease called polio. Polio is caused by a **virus** which attacks and destroys the nerve cells. This can cause **paralysis** and means that the patient may never be able to move an arm or leg again.

Joints can become red, swollen, and painful from a disease called arthritis. Many people with arthritis need a cane or a walking frame to help them get around. Others are confined to wheelchairs.

29

In the Hospital

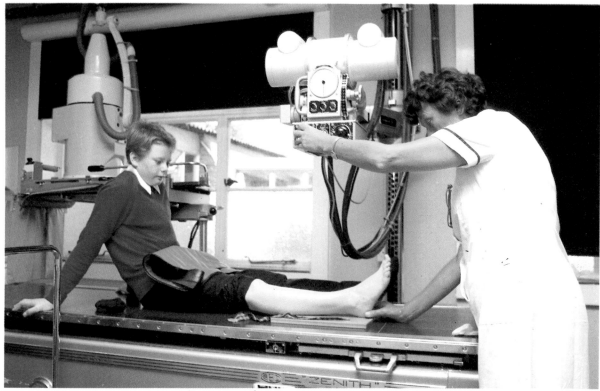

The child in our picture is having an **X ray** of his leg so that the doctor can see how badly it is broken. The light of the X ray can look right through the skin to the bones inside.

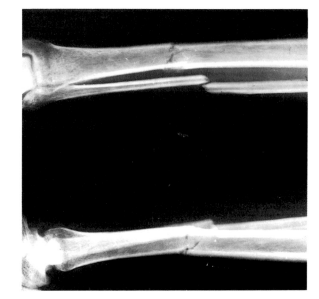

an X-ray picture of a broken tibia and fibula

30

If the bones are broken into many pieces, an **orthopedic surgeon** may need to cut the body open to pin or screw the bones back into position. During the operation, everything must be kept spotlessly clean and free from **germs.**

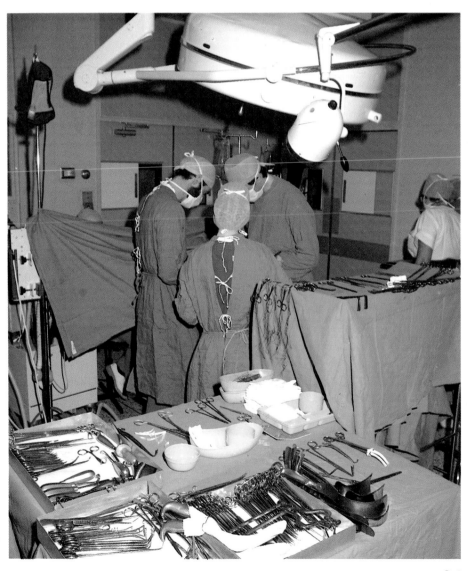

Made to Measure

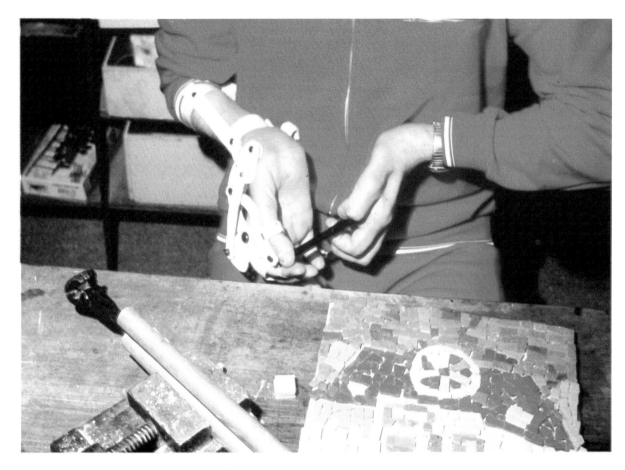

Sometimes joints become so painful that it is difficult to move them. The picture shows a patient whose hands have become twisted and bent. He has been given something that helps him to use his hands to pick things up and make pictures.

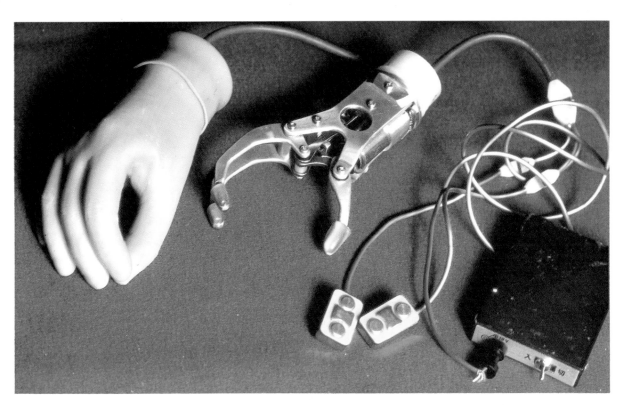

When a limb has been **amputated,** the patient can be given an **artificial limb** instead. Engineers use electronics and plastics to build an artificial hand or leg, which is attached firmly. It may take the patient two or three months to learn to use the new limb.

using an artificial leg

Getting Around

Many disabled people use wheelchairs or specially-adapted cars.

Homes and offices need to be carefully planned so that everything can be reached from the wheelchair.

Athletes need strong arm muscles for a wheelchair race.

a kitchen
with
everything
at the right
height for
someone in
a wheelchair

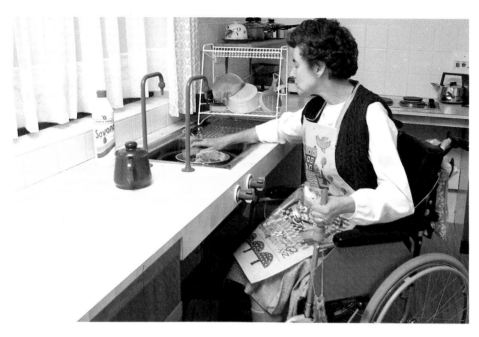

a wheelchair
race

On the Move Again

If you break a bone, or are sick in bed for a long time, your muscles get weak. Exercise helps to build up weak muscles. Machines can also help the body to start moving again.

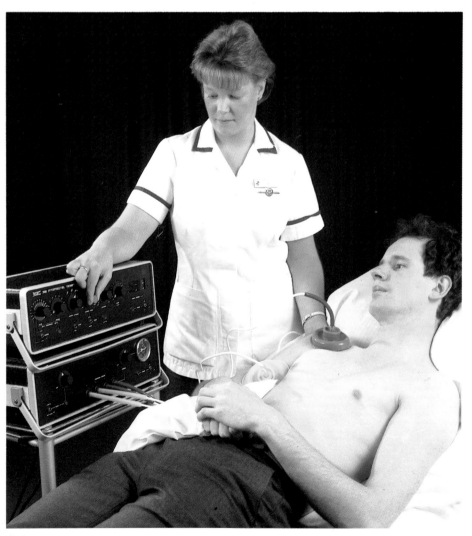

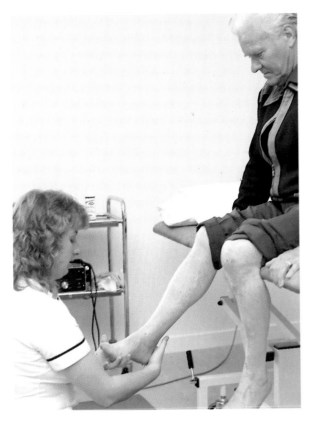

A **physical therapist** helps patients make their weak muscles and limbs strong. The physical therapist checks movement in a limb and chooses the exercises to strengthen muscles.

A swimming pool is an ideal place to strengthen muscles because the limbs do not feel so heavy. This makes it easier to move the weak limbs.

water helps this patient strengthen his weak muscles

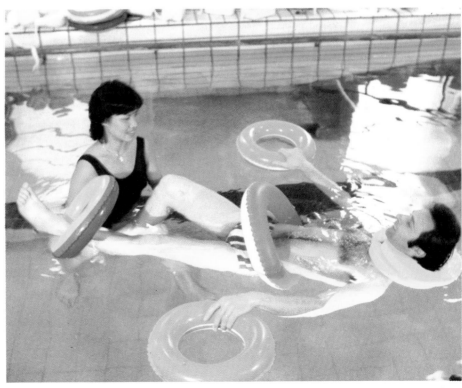

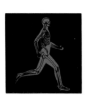

First Aid

If someone has fallen and broken a bone, keep calm and call an adult or phone for an ambulance right away. Do not let the person try to move.

Tying a Sling

knot

safety pin

a triangular bandage helps to support a broken arm

You may have to wait a while for help. If you have a coat or blanket, put it over the injured person and try to keep them warm.

Groups like the Red Cross run courses to teach people first aid and what to do in an emergency.

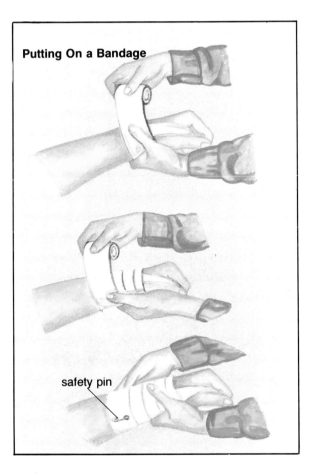

Putting On a Bandage

safety pin

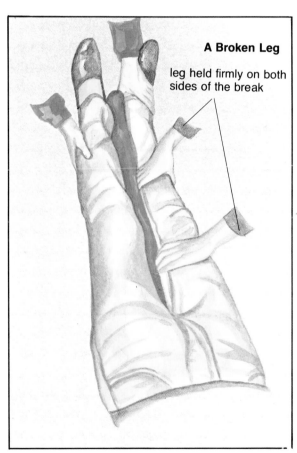

A Broken Leg

leg held firmly on both sides of the break

a bandage can be used to support a sprained ankle or wrist

do not move a broken leg but support it with something soft under it

Body Fuel

When a little boy named Eric eats bananas, he changes into the cartoon character of Bananaman. He becomes big and strong. Fruit and vegetables contain **vitamins** and minerals to help keep you healthy.

milk gives us a good supply of calcium

Milk contains **calcium** that we need
to strengthen our bones and teeth.
Butter, cream, milk, cheese, and nuts
contain fats that provide **energy.**

People in some parts of the world
cannot get enough food to eat. The
hungry family in this picture is waiting
for a plane to arrive with food
supplies.

Keeping Fit

You need regular, gentle exercise to keep fit.

Your muscles use **oxygen.** When you breathe in, oxygen goes to your lungs. Your heart pumps it around your body in your blood. Exercise strengthens your heart and lungs.

people puff and pant after a race to get more oxygen into their lungs

By training every day, you can build up your muscles until they are huge. You do not need huge muscles to be fit and well.

The chart shows different kinds of sports which help you to keep fit in different ways.

Swimming is the best all-around exercise. It strengthens the heart and lungs, strengthens the muscles, and keeps most of the joints supple.

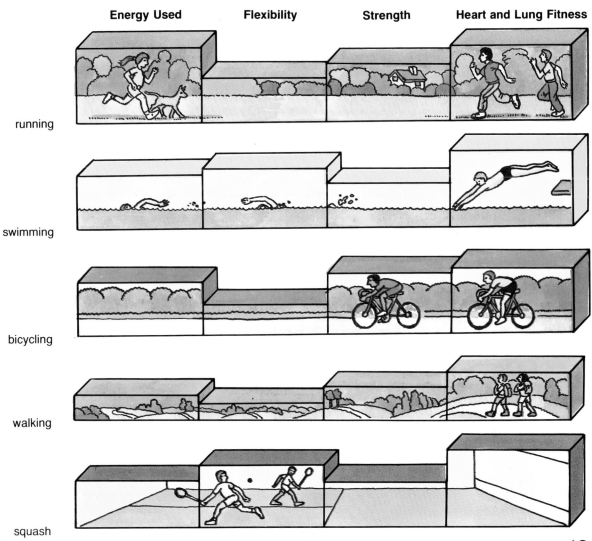

| Energy Used | Flexibility | Strength | Heart and Lung Fitness |

running

swimming

bicycling

walking

squash

A Changing World

Our bodies were not designed to sit in chairs all day long. Our bodies were designed so we could run fast, walk long distances, throw stones and spears, carry heavy objects, and shoot an arrow like the native hunter in the picture.

Years ago people walked to work. Now we use escalators, elevators, trains, and cars.

Astronauts find that their bones lose calcium when they spend long periods in weightless conditions.

In the future, if we spend a lot of time in space, our bodies might begin to change shape.

these astronauts are weightless inside their space capsule

Glossary

amputate   to cut off a limb, especially an arm or a leg.

artificial limb   an arm, a leg, a foot, or a hand that has been made in a factory.

astronauts   people who are trained to fly in spacecraft.

ball-and-socket joint   a joint made by a round knob moving freely in a cup-shaped holder.

blood vessels   tubes that carry blood around your body.

brain   the "computer" in our heads that controls what we do.

calcium   a substance found in green vegetables and foods such as milk and cheese, which we need for healthy bones, teeth, and muscles.

callus   the material that forms while a break in a bone heals.

cartilage   a tough, rubbery material that protects the ends of bones.

cell   a very small part or unit.

cranium   the bones of the head that protect the brain.

digest   to break down food so it can be used by the body.

energy   the power to do work.

fibrous joint   a joint in which the bones are attached firmly together by fibers, which allow little or no movement.

fibula   the thin bone at the back of the lower leg.

germ   a tiny living thing that can cause disease.

gliding joint   a joint where two flat surfaces move over one another.

gray matter   a substance in the brain and the center of the spinal cord, where nerves bring messages from the body and take back instructions to the muscles.

hinge joint   a joint where movement is only backward and forward, like a door.

involuntary   something that happens automatically, without thought.

ligament   a strip of rubbery material that holds the two bones of a joint together.

marrow   the soft, fatty substance in the middle of bones where blood cells are made.

minerals   natural substances found in the ground that are not formed from plant or animal life.

muscle   a type of material in the body that can shorten itself to produce movement.

nerves   a network of tiny "cables" that pass messages from all parts of the body to the brain and back again.

orthopedic surgeon   a doctor who cures illnesses by operating on the skeleton.

oxygen   a gas found in air and water. We cannot breathe without oxygen.

paralysis   loss of movement or feeling.

patella   the bone that covers the front of the knee joint.

physical therapist   someone who treats muscles and bones by using heat, massage, or exercises.

radius   the outer bone in the lower arm that lies between the elbow and the thumb.

red blood cell   a part of the blood that carries oxygen.

rib   one of the bones in your chest.

skull   the bones that make up the head of an animal.

spinal cord   the string of fibers that runs down the inside of the spine.

spine   the line of small bones that runs down the length of the back of all vertebrates.

splint   a rigid piece of material for holding a broken bone in place.

stirrup   one of the three tiny bones inside the ear.

tendon   a band of tough material that joins muscles to the bones in the body.

tibia   the shin bone, found at the front of the lower leg.

traction   the act of pulling. Weights are used to pull muscles and keep broken bones in place.

ulna   the inner bone of the arm that leads from the elbow toward the little finger side of the wrist.

vertebrae   the line of small bones found down the center of the back of vertebrates.

virus   a kind of germ that causes disease when it gets inside the body's cells.

vitamins   substances found in foods such as vegetables and fruit that are needed for good health and growth.

voluntary   something that does not happen automatically, but which is controlled by thought.

white matter   a substance in the outer layer of the spinal cord that carries messages to and from the brain.

X ray   a light ray that can be used to photograph parts of the body from the outside.

Index

© Heinemann Children's Reference 1990
Artwork © BLA Publishing Limited 1987
Material used in this book first appeared in Macmillan World Library: *How Our Bodies Work: The Skeleton and Movement*. Published by Heinemann Children's Reference.